HITLER

BETWEEN

· THE ·

WARS

1918-1939

THE ARMISTICE
AND AFTER

❋

John C. Miles

W
FRANKLIN WATTS
LONDON · SYDNEY

Franklin Watts

First published in Great Britain in 2017 by The Watts Publishing Group

Project Editor: Sarah Silver
Editor: Sarah Ridley
Designer: Darren Jordan
Cover Designer: Peter Scoulding
Picture Researcher: Diana Morris

ISBN 978 1 4451 5060 4

Printed in China

Franklin Watts
An imprint of
Hachette Children's Group
Part of The Watts Publishing Group
Carmelite House
50 Victoria Embankment
London EC4Y 0DZ

An Hachette UK Company
www.hachette.co.uk

www.franklinwatts.co.uk

Picture acknowledgements
The publisher would like to thank the following for permission to
reproduce their pictures:

Apic/Hulton Archive/Getty Images: 19tc. George Grantham Bain/LOC/CC
Wikimedia Commons: 19cr. Bettmann/Getty Image: front cover l, 2-3, 25,41l.
Bibliotheque Nationale de France/cc Wikimedia Commons: 14bl. Central
Press/Hulton Archive/Getty Images: 39c. Corbis Historical/Hulton Deutsch/
Getty Images: 21b. Ian Dagnall Computing/Alamy: 26. Mary Evans PL/Alamy:
23cr. Everett Collection/Alamy: 4. Everett Historical/Shutterstock: front cover
tr, 5,8, 13cr, 27b, 30, 31r, 39t, 43cr. Firmin/Hulton Archive/Getty Images:
20bl. Fox Photos/Hulton Archive/Getty Images: 38. FPG/Hulton Archive/
Getty Images: 35b. French official photographer/Imperial War Museum: 11.
Granger Historical Archive/Alamy: 29r,36, 42. Hulton Archive/Getty Images:
43tl. Imperial War Museum: 20tr. Interfoto/Alamy: 28. ITAR-TASS/Alamy: 17bl.
Edward N Jackson. US Army Signal Corps./CC Wikimedia Commons: 12.
Keystone/Hulton Archive/Getty Images: 34. League of Nations Photo Archive:
15cl. 2nd Lieutenant David McLellan/Imperial War Museum: 10. Mondardori
Portfolio/Getty Images: 22, 23bl. Christian Mueller/Shutterstock: 41r. National
Archives/CC Wikimedia Commons: 31l. Courtesy of André Rondeau, Metari
Stamps: 6tr. Elzbieta Sekowska/Shutterstock: front cover br. TASS/Topfoto:
33r. Topfoto: 33l. Eddie Toro/Dreamstime: 27t. UIG/Getty Images: 35t. Ulstein
Bild/Getty Images: 37br, 40. Underwood Archives/Getty Images: 24. Walter Art
Museum, Baltimore/Wikimedia Commons: 6bl. CC Wikimedia Commons:
7bl, 9, 13bl, 14br, 15cr, 16, 17cr, 19tr, 29l, 32. ysuel/Shutterstock: front cover c.

909.822

CONTENTS

CONSEQUENCES OF WAR

Between 1914 and 1918, people across the world were fighting the worst war that civilisation had ever seen. This deadly conflict killed and injured millions in new and terrible ways and caused untold misery and hardship. At the time, many people called this war 'The Great War' – 'great' as in massive and all-encompassing. It also became known as 'the war to end all wars', in the hope that political leaders would choose peace over war in the future. Today we call this conflict the First World War or World War I.

Below: First World War tactics included bombardment by heavy artillery (huge field guns), which caused millions of casualties (injured and dead). Here three howitzers of the Royal Garrison Artillery fire on German trenches during the Battle of the Somme, 1916.

The huge upheavals caused by the events of 1914–18 resulted in some radical systems of government being tried out. One of these, communism, was established by revolution in Russia. Communist governments continued to control Russia, renamed the Soviet Union, until the late 20th century.

Across Europe, the treaties that ended the First World War, including the Treaty of Versailles, caused much unrest. The terms imposed by these treaties, as well as poor leadership and the effects of the 1929 economic depression, were exploited by extremist political parties, such as the Nazis, to popularise their beliefs. These beliefs were based on hatred and finding scapegoats for their countries' woes.

Above: During the 1930s, the National Socialist Workers' Party (Nazis) held elaborate rallies and ceremonies where they repeated their ideas and beliefs, aiming to unite Germans into a disciplined, unstoppable nation capable of conquering other countries.

This book examines how the horrors of four years of total war were finally ended. It focuses on the treaties signed by former enemies and the far-reaching consequences of those treaties, consequences that were partly to blame for another catastrophic war 20 years later. Understanding these historical events might help nations to avoid making similar mistakes in the future for, in the words of the philosopher George Santayana, 'Those who cannot remember the past are condemned to repeat it.'

THE FIRST WORLD WAR

For more than four years the First World War had raged around the world, claiming millions of lives. But what had caused the war, and who was fighting whom?

Below: This 1898 Canadian stamp shows the British Empire in red, demonstrating just how much of the world Britain governed.

Industry, empires and power

In the 1800s, Great Britain, France, Germany, Austria-Hungary and Russia developed into wealthy nations based on finance, industry and the manufacture of goods. But with increasing riches came great rivalry. European countries rushed to expand their worldwide colonial empires, using strong armies and navies to back up their claims.

The rise of Germany

In the short Franco-Prussian War of 1870–71, the powerful Germanic state of Prussia inflicted a humiliating defeat on France and claimed the territory of Alsace-Lorraine. This victory helped to complete the process of unifying German states into a single German nation in 1871. Led by Kaiser (Emperor) Wilhelm I and statesman Otto von Bismarck, this new, united Germany altered the balance of power within Europe.

Disastrous alliances

By 1914 the most powerful countries in Europe were divided into two groups. Within

Left: Portrait of the Prussian politician Otto von Bismarck.

each group, nations had signed alliances and treaties agreeing to support each other if attacked. On one side were the Allies – France, Russia, Britain and the British Empire; opposing them were the Central Powers – Germany and Austria-Hungary. Many smaller nations were part of this complicated web of alliances. (Turn to page 44 for a map of Europe at this time.)

War begins

On 28 June 1914, Archduke Franz Ferdinand, heir to the throne of Austria-Hungary, was assassinated in Sarajevo, Bosnia. Over the next 37 days, decisions made by European leaders led to war. First Austria-Hungary declared war on Serbia, triggering Europe's network of alliances to come into play. Russia had promised to protect Serbia so it declared war on Austria-Hungary. Germany, bound to support Austria-Hungary, and fearing attacks from France or Russia, invaded neutral Belgium on its way to France, bringing Britain into the war to defend Belgium. The war had begun.

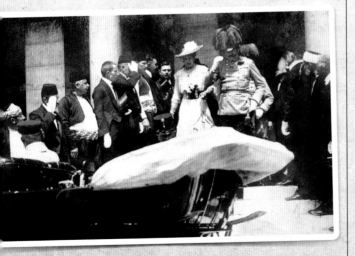

Above: Archduke Franz Ferdinand and Duchess Sophie visit Sarajevo in Bosnia on 28 June 1914. Shortly after this photo was taken they were shot dead by Gavrilo Princip, a Bosnian Serb.

The course of the war

The advance of the German army towards Paris was stopped in Belgium and northern France with the help of British soldiers. Troops on both sides dug themselves into protective trenches. Warfare on this 'Western Front' stayed much the same until 1917. On the 'Eastern Front', Russia fought against both Germany and Austria-Hungary. Late in 1914, the Central Powers were joined by the Ottoman Empire, based in Turkey, opening up new theatres of war in the Middle East. Italy and Japan joined the Allied cause in 1915.

Above: This map shows the main theatres of war in Europe. Fighting occurred across the globe, including the Middle East, parts of Africa and out at sea.

After the Bolshevik revolution of 1917 (see pages 16–17), the government of Russia collapsed. The Treaty of Brest-Litovsk (see page 8), signed in March 1918, ended Russia's war with the Central Powers. Meanwhile, the entry of the USA into the war in 1917 on the Allied side had brought US soldiers and military equipment into the conflict, hastening the end of the war in late 1918.

THE FIGHTING ENDS

In March 1918, the German army launched a tactically brilliant offensive on the Western Front, gaining much territory. However, by mid-August 1918, the tables had turned and the Allies were beginning to win the war. But coming up with a workable plan to end the war involved complicated and delicate negotiations.

Wilson's 'Fourteen Points'

Back in April 1917, US President Woodrow Wilson had asked the US Congress to declare war on Germany to 'make the world safe for democracy'. In January 1918 he made another speech in which he outlined the 'Fourteen Points' – the USA's wish list for the post-war world. These included an end to secret diplomacy, freedom of trade, a reduction in weapons and the right to democracy for peoples who had been the subjects of pre-war empires. Wilson also called for the founding of an international peace-keeping organisation.

TREATY OF BREST-LITOVSK

The Treaty of Brest-Litovsk between Soviet Russia and the Central Powers was signed on 3 March 1918, formally ending Russia's participation in the war. The new Bolshevik government wanted to concentrate on their own country, but the terms they agreed to were harsh. Soviet Russia had to give the Baltic states to Germany and the province of Kars Oblast in the Caucasus region to the Ottoman Empire. It also had to recognise the independence of the Ukraine region, which was to be a new country under German protection. In total Soviet Russia lost a quarter of its population and industry, including nearly all its coal mines. For Germany, alongside the territorial gains, it no longer had to fight a war on two fronts and could focus on the Western Front.

Left: US President Woodrow Wilson

Chaos in Germany

By late summer 1918 Germany was exhausted and in the grip of a severe economic and political crisis. At the end of September both Kaiser Wilhelm II and the German military leaders realised that there was no chance of victory. German general Erich Ludendorff recommended asking the Allies for a ceasefire. He also advised setting up a democratic parliamentary-style government.

On 5 October, Germany announced that it was prepared to negotiate an armistice based on Wilson's 'Fourteen Points'. Reaction from the rest of the Allied powers to this development was lukewarm as many of the 'Fourteen Points' didn't fit in with their plans for the post-war world. French politicians, in particular, wanted revenge on Germany for the damage the war had done to their country.

On 29 October, events in Germany took a turn for the worse as rebellion broke out in the key port of Kiel. Sailors, soldiers and workers were demanding an end to the monarchy. As unrest began to spread and increasing numbers of soldiers deserted from the German army, Kaiser Wilhelm II finally abdicated and went into exile.

Signing the Armistice

The new German government sent a delegation to France to negotiate an armistice, or peace agreement. The Germans were given a list of Allied demands, which included a ceasefire to take effect within six hours of the signing, the withdrawal of German forces from all occupied territories, abandoning gains from the Treaty of Brest-Litovsk with Russia (see box), the handing over of German war supplies and weapons and the release of Allied prisoners of war. With no question of negotiation, Germany finally signed the Armistice at 5.20 am on 11 November 1918.

As the day dawned the war went on as usual; 2,738 men were killed before the ceasefire at 11 am that morning. The mood in the Allied trenches was subdued, but in Paris and London crowds burst into wild celebrations when the end of the fighting was officially announced.

Left: *The German delegation (left) prepares to sign the Armistice in French military leader Ferdinand Foch's private railway carriage. Foch, dressed in the blue uniform, stands on the right.*

COUNTING THE COST

When the Armistice took effect at 11 am on 11 November 1918, the slaughter finally stopped. The world could begin to add up the cost of the war.

Killed, wounded, disabled

The cost of the war in human lives was shocking. Approximately 65 million men fought in the conflict; of these 8.5 million were killed and 21.2 million injured. Exact totals will never be known, so these figures can only remain estimates. In many countries almost an entire generation of young men was killed; millions more were disabled for life.

Most families were mourning the loss of at least one son, father or brother; some lost all their male relatives. Many soldiers who fought returned from the war with horrific injuries, both physical and mental. The technology that allowed machine guns to fire more than 500 rounds a minute meant that army medical staff had to work very hard to deal with some of the injuries sustained by soldiers. In addition, 'shell-shock' or, as we would term it today, 'post-traumatic stress disorder', affected millions of men who had experienced events that no human being should have to face.

Between the warring countries the total number of deaths varied considerably. Both Germany and Russia lost 1.7 million men each; Britain and its empire lost more than 950,000. In addition to the deaths of soldiers, more than six million civilians were killed. Two million Russians died of starvation and another one million Armenians were wiped out in a campaign of genocide against them by Ottoman forces.

Left: *Members of the Women's Auxiliary Army Corps tend British war graves at Abbeville, France. All warring nations had the massive task of creating cemeteries and erecting gravestones and memorials.*

The economic cost

In 1914 no country was prepared for a total war. As fighting increased and more soldiers and war supplies were needed, governments had to take extreme measures that affected the lives of everyone. In Britain, for example, the government took control of the nation's economy. It set up arms factories, limited imports so that more British products were bought and conscripted men who might otherwise have been working in industry to go and fight. British women stepped in and replaced workers in what had been all-male occupations. The end of the war presented great challenges in Britain and across Europe as countries struggled to get their peace-time economies working.

In financial terms the cost of the war was staggering to both the defeated nations and the victors. For instance, in September 1918, the cost to Britain for only one day's ammunition was £3.87 million, or more than £191 million today. The entire war cost Britain £3.25 billion – more than £161 billion in today's money. Taxes had to be raised to pay for this and in Britain the national debt increased tenfold. The same was true for countries across Europe.

Below: The devastated French town of Béthune in 1918. In countries where the war had been fought, entire cities and towns had to be rebuilt and local farmland needed to be cleared of military equipment, shells and explosives.

THE TREATY OF VERSAILLES

After the ceasefire in November 1918, it took many months for world leaders to agree the terms of the treaties that officially ended the First World War. The Treaty of Versailles was the formal agreement that concluded the war with Germany.

Right: The 'Big Four' (left to right): Prime Minister David Lloyd George of Britain, Prime Minister Vittorio Orlando of Italy, Prime Minister Georges Clemenceau of France and President Woodrow Wilson of the USA decided upon the main terms agreed at the Paris Peace Conference.

Getting the treaty to the table

The treaty contained a series of demands that aimed to disable Germany as a military power and make it pay for the devastation of more than four years of all-out war. Discussions to draft the document began in Paris on 18 January 1919 between delegates from 27 nations.

Punishment

The treaty dealt harshly with a defeated Germany. Among other demands, it stripped the country of 65,000 sq km of territory, including land gained through the Treaty of Brest-Litovsk (see page 8). Germany had to recognise the independence of Poland and Czechoslovakia and to surrender control of its former colonies around the world. It was required to turn over the production of its Saar region's coal mines to France for 15 years to compensate that country for having wrecked its coal production.

Militarily, Germany had to destroy or hand over its war supplies, most of its navy, limit any future army to no more than 100,000 men and disband its air force entirely. In addition, Germany had to agree to accept 'war guilt' (see box) and to pay reparations of 132 billion gold marks to the Allies – a truly enormous sum, equivalent to roughly £284 billion today.

Getting Germany to sign

Reaction in Germany to the Treaty of Versailles was, unsurprisingly, negative. Article 231 caused particular offence, as German leaders believed it to be an unacceptable slur on national honour. Nevertheless, the agreement was presented by the Allies as a non-negotiable deal.

The treaty's terms faced so much opposition within Germany that the democratically elected head of the first post-war government, Philipp Scheidemann, resigned. Scheidemann's successor, Gustav Bauer, tried in vain to get certain clauses removed from the treaty. Eventually the Allies issued Bauer with an ultimatum – if Germany refused to sign, Allied forces would invade within 24 hours. Faced with this nightmare scenario, Bauer sent a telegram to French leader Georges Clemenceau telling him that Germany would sign the treaty.

Above: International delegates gathered in the Hall of Mirrors in the Palace of Versailles to sign the treaty.

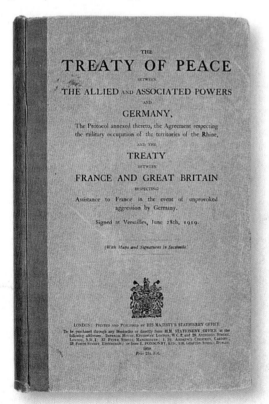

Above: The Treaty of Versailles consisted of 440 articles setting out the terms of the settlement. It was signed on 28 June 1919.

ARTICLE 231 – WAR GUILT

One of the most controversial demands in the Treaty of Versailles was Article 231, which defined Germany as a violent aggressor by requiring it to 'accept the responsibility of Germany and her allies for causing all the loss and damage' of the war. This became known as the 'War Guilt' clause. Other former members of the Central Powers were required to sign similar articles.

THE POST-WAR WORLD

The Treaty of Versailles had begun the process of redrawing the map of the post-war world; similar treaties with other members of the former Central Powers followed. The Paris Peace Conference also established a new worldwide peacekeeping organisation called the League of Nations.

Austria, Bulgaria, Hungary

In September 1919, the Treaty of St Germain with Austria created the German-speaking Republic of Austria, which, like Germany, had to pay war reparations. Some Austrian territory was given to neighbours and the country was forbidden to unite with Germany. The Treaty of Neuilly with Bulgaria, signed in November 1919, allocated land to Greece and Yugoslavia and forced Bulgaria to pay war reparations. In June 1920 the Treaty of Trianon with Hungary again imposed war reparations, reduced that country to two-thirds of its former size and gave territory to surrounding nations (see map, page 44).

The Ottoman Empire and Turkey

The Treaty of Sèvres was signed between the Allies and the Ottoman Empire in August 1920. It stripped the Empire of its Arab lands and gave western Turkey to Greece. However, this treaty was rejected by the new republican government of Turkey and was replaced by the Treaty of Lausanne in June 1923, which returned the Greek gain to Turkey and recognised Turkey's new borders.

Right: Kemal Ataturk, founder of the Turkish Republic in 1923 and its first president.

Left: Delegates arriving for the signing of the Treaty of Trianon.

The League of Nations

Initially envisaged by President Woodrow Wilson of the USA, the determination to establish a forum for resolving international disputes grew out of the worldwide reaction to the horrors of the war. The league came into being on 28 June 1919, when 44 of the countries attending the Paris Peace Conference signed the agreement establishing it. The league's headquarters were in Geneva, Switzerland.

Above: League of Nations meeting in Geneva, Switzerland in 1920.

Functions of the league included safeguarding the borders of member states, taking action to maintain peace and promoting worldwide disarmament. The league was also tasked with establishing governments in territories, such as Palestine and Syria, that had once belonged to the Central Powers.

Although the league was President Wilson's idea, many US politicians feared American membership of it would lead to further involvement in European politics. As a result, a key domestic vote to ratify the USA's membership was defeated, and one of the world's most powerful countries never joined the League of Nations.

Problems of the League of Nations

One of the main weaknesses of the league was that it lacked an army capable of enforcing its resolutions. Its commitment to the idea that everyone should act together to maintain peace would require some member states to take unpopular actions against countries they might otherwise consider friendly.

The weaknesses of the league became increasingly clear in the 1930s, when it was unable to take effective action against aggressive nations such as Japan (see pages 36–37). By then some politicians were beginning to realise that the dream of disarmament, so popular after the First World War, was practically impossible.

Above: This cartoon printed in 1919 depicts the League of Nations muzzling 'the dog of war'. It reflects early hopes about what the league might be able to achieve in terms of preserving world peace.

RUSSIAN REVOLUTIONS

The outcome of the Russian revolutions in 1917 affected both the First World War and politics for much of the 20th century. But why were there revolutions in Russia in the first place?

Tsarist Russia

Russia in the late 1800s was a society strictly organised by social class. Nicholas II, who became tsar (emperor) in 1894, led an elite that tightly ruled the country. Russia's rapid industrialisation from around 1890 had brought many changes as people flocked to cities to take up factory jobs. But with no say in government, workers believed that Russian society had to change. They set up 'soviets', or workers' councils, to further their aims, and protests and strikes against poor conditions increased every year.

Above: Tsar Nicholas II, pictured with his daughters on the imperial yacht. They would all be murdered by the Bolsheviks in 1918.

Events came to a head in 1905, when hundreds of protesters were shot dead by Tsarist troops. The revolution that resulted from this did bring about some reform – Tsar Nicholas promised to allow an elected assembly. However, the powers of this body were limited and unrest continued to grow. By 1914 Tsar Nicholas and his family were seen by many Russians as incompetent and corrupt.

Russia goes to war

The First World War was devastating for Russia, whose armed forces suffered heavy losses. The Russian army lacked weapons, clothing and munitions. By October 1916 nearly two million men had died in the armed forces; another two million had been taken prisoner. As the Russian economy began to crack under the strain, food became scarce and crime dramatically increased.

The 1917 revolutions

By February 1917 Russia was at breaking point. Strikes closed factories and the streets of Petrograd (St Petersburg) filled with demonstrators, many of whom focused their anger on the royal family. The Tsar ordered troops to crush the unrest but the soldiers refused. Eventually, on 15 March, Tsar Nicholas abdicated and soon after, a moderate provisional government was formed. But this lacked support and was, in turn, toppled by a second small but well-organised revolution in October 1917. This was headed by Vladimir Lenin, the leader of the radical communist Bolshevik Party. Lenin's revolution replaced the provisional government with a communist government. It was this new government that signed the Treaty of Brest-Litovsk with Germany on 3 March 1918, ending Russia's involvement in the First World War.

Above: Street fighting breaks out in Petrograd in July 1917 during the unrest in the months following the February Revolution.

Civil war

By 1918, a divided Russia had descended into a bitter civil war in which the Bolshevik Red Army fought the White Army made up of liberal and monarchist Russian forces. The White Army was backed by powers such as Great Britain and France who feared the establishment of communism in Russia. But by 1923, the White Army forces were defeated and the Bolsheviks had gradually taken control. Communism had triumphed.

Above: Bolshevik leader Vladimir Lenin addresses troops in Moscow on 25 May 1919. The Bolshevik message of 'Peace, land and bread' appealed to millions of ordinary Russians.

COMMUNISM

Communism's doctrine of putting power and property in the hands of ordinary people appealed strongly to workers in many countries who felt exploited by industrialists, bankers and the ruling elite. After 1917, communists aimed to transform the whole world into communist states. As the events of the 20th century unfolded, the governments of many nations remained deeply fearful of communism, which they perceived as a dangerous threat to their own power.

PROBLEMS IN THE MIDDLE EAST

The signing of the Treaty of Sèvres on 10 August 1920 began the process of splitting up the defeated Ottoman Empire. Non-Turkish former Ottoman territories were handed over to the victorious Allies to govern. But conflicting promises made by Britain helped lay the foundations of today's Middle Eastern conflicts.

The Sykes-Picot agreement

In 1916 Britain and France formulated the Sykes-Picot agreement. This proposed that, in the event of the Allies winning the First World War, former provinces of the Ottoman Empire in the Middle East would be divided into 'spheres of influence' and control. Britain would control the coastal strip between the Mediterranean Sea and the River Jordan, Jordan and southern Iraq, as well as the ports of Haifa and Acre. France would control southeastern Turkey, northern Iraq, Syria and Lebanon. After the end of the war the League of Nations awarded 'mandates' for Britain and France to govern territories covered by the agreement. For Britain, this included Palestine – a land populated mainly by Muslim Arabs.

This seemed good news for the Arabs who had supported Britain in its war with the Ottoman Empire. Britain had made promises to Arab leaders that, in the event of victory, it would support the creation of an Arab national homeland in Palestine. But there was a problem.

Zionism

Throughout the 1800s and early 1900s, support had grown in both Europe and the

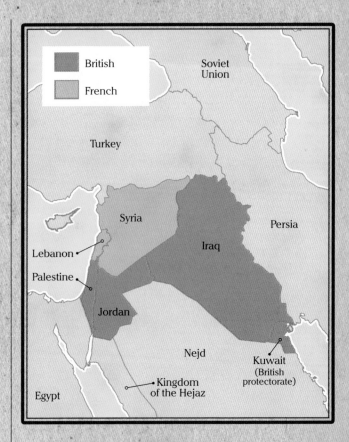

Above: *This map shows the areas of control in 1923, as originally set out by the Sykes-Picot agreement. Syria, Lebanon, Iraq and Jordan had been part of the Ottoman Empire.*

USA for the establishment of a homeland for the Jewish people in Palestine, centred around Jerusalem – land which Jews believe had been granted to them by God. This movement, Zionism, gathered momentum as wave after wave of persecution in countries such as Tsarist Russia killed or displaced millions of Jews.

Conflicting promises?

By 1916 Zionist leader Chaim Weizmann had met with Prime Minister David Lloyd George of Britain and his foreign secretary, Arthur Balfour, setting forth his vision for a Jewish homeland in Palestine. Both politicians viewed Weizmann's plan favourably. To Muslim leader Hussein bin Ali, Sharif of Mecca, however, this action contradicted the promises Britain was making to Arabs in return for their help in the war against Ottoman forces.

The Balfour Declaration

In November 1917, Balfour sent a letter to Walter Rothschild, a leader of Britain's Jewish community. It stated:

> *His Majesty's government view with favour the establishment in Palestine of a national home for the Jewish people, and will use their best endeavours to facilitate the achievement of this object.*

By sending this declaration that supported Zionist aspirations, Lloyd George and Balfour hoped to attract Jewish financial support for the war and appeal to Jews around the world to support the Allied war effort.

What happened next?

In 1920, Britain was granted its mandate to govern Palestine, and a post-war military occupation was replaced with a civil government. Large numbers of Jews began to emigrate to Palestine. However, conflict

Above left: Zionist leader, Chaim Weizmann

Above right: Hussein bin Ali, Sharif of Mecca, launched an Arab revolt against the Ottoman Turks in 1916 to help Britain.

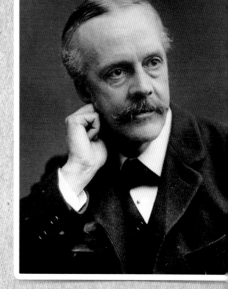

Right: British Foreign Secretary, Arthur Balfour

soon began to arise between Palestinian Arabs and Jews, resulting in serious riots. These were badly handled by the British administration and, as a result, Palestinian Arabs refused to co-operate with any organisation that included Jews. The two communities now living in Palestine were set on conflicting and seemingly irreconcilable paths.

BRITAIN IN THE 1920s

What life was like in 1920s Britain depended very much on who you were. For many of the middle and upper classes, the 1920s were a fun time. Ordinary working people, however, faced housing shortages, unemployment and hardship.

After the war

Many former soldiers found civilian life difficult. Hundreds of thousands were returning to the job market, but employment was scarce in many areas and huge numbers of men had experienced life-changing injuries. The British government granted war pensions to military personnel, merchant seamen and nurses who had served. These included disability pensions for those who had been injured and incomes for the widows of men who had been killed in action or who had later died of their wounds.

Above: A disabled ex-serviceman makes furniture at a Lord Roberts Memorial Workshop. By 1920 there were 11 workshops across the country, offering training to men injured during the war.

1920s life

The war had been good to some people, such as the wealthy owners of factories who had supplied war materials to the armed services. For well-off young people, the 1920s was a time to celebrate life after a war in which so many of their friends had been killed. Many young people pursued a fun-seeking lifestyle in the nightclubs of London and other large cities. Jazz music, imported from the USA, became very popular.

Left: Elegantly dressed 1920s couples dance the night away at a rooftop party at the Criterion, London.

'Homes fit for heroes'

The end of the war created a huge demand for housing. In 1919 the British government passed the Addison Act, which promised to build 500,000 'homes fit for heroes' within three years. The act was significant as it made housing a national responsibility. However, a weakening economy meant that only 213,000 homes were actually built. By the mid-1920s there was a desperate housing shortage; but from 1924 local councils were given government money to clear poor-quality housing and gradually build 700,000 new homes.

Economic woes

By the mid-1920s the British economy was in trouble. The Chancellor of the Exchequer, Winston Churchill, reintroduced the 'gold standard' in 1925. This linked the British pound sterling to its value in gold and meant that British-made goods became expensive and hard to sell abroad. Interest rates rose and, with industrial output falling, wages fell too, creating hardship. Britain's booming economy of the early post-war years had gone bust, foreshadowing the economic depression of the 1930s (see pages 26–27).

THE GENERAL STRIKE

In the 1920s Britain was struggling economically as a result of the huge cost of the First World War. This cut the profits paid to the owners of many industries. In 1926, coal mine owners tried to keep their profits high by reducing miners' wages. As a protest, Britain's trade unions called a general strike. Between 4–13 May nearly two million miners, railwaymen, dockers and other workers stopped work. However the government had been planning for this and recruited volunteers to try and keep essential services running. Eventually a court case ruled that most of the trade unions were acting illegally and the strike was called off. Some miners continued to strike until lack of money forced them back to work; others remained unemployed for years.

Left: *A protest march in Crewe during the 1926 General Strike.*

FASCISM IN ITALY

The treaties that ended the First World War left the Italians, who had fought on the Allied side, feeling hard done by. Their discontent paved the way for the rise of the first of the dictators to seize power in the 1920s and 30s.

A unified country

Like Germany, until the mid-1800s Italy had been a collection of smaller states. In 1861 it united as a constitutional monarchy, in which a king ruled with the assistance of parliament. Although Italy possessed a much smaller colonial empire than some other European powers, it had some colonies, including the North African country of Libya which it seized from the Ottoman Empire in 1912.

First World War

Italy joined the war in 1915, mainly fighting Austro-Hungarian forces in the mountainous regions to the north and east of the Adriatic Sea. For Italy the conflict was very costly – more than 700,000 servicemen died and the Italian economy wound up heavily in debt. At the end of the war Italy had been promised new territory but had actually gained little from the peace treaties. Discontent turned to civil unrest when Italian radical forces took control of part of what is now Slovenia in 1919.

The rise of Mussolini

Benito Mussolini came to prominence before the First World War as a member of the left-wing Italian Socialist Party where he promoted revolutionary ideas. A passionate speaker, Mussolini served with the army during the war and was wounded. By 1919 he had moved away from his left-wing views and had founded the Fasci di Combattimento (Combat League). The Fasci wore black-shirted uniforms and fought violently with left-wing socialist opponents.

Left: *Italian troops on the move. They battled with Austria-Hungary's forces during the First World War in very difficult mountainous conditions, coping with deep snow in the winters.*

By 1921 Mussolini had turned his group into the National Fascist Party. Taking advantage of seething discontent and a 1922 general strike, Fascist Party supporters staged a mass march on Rome, where Mussolini demanded that the king make him prime minister. King Victor Emmanuel III was in a difficult position – he feared civil war and had to choose between the pro-monarchy Fascist Party or the anti-monarchy Socialist Party. He chose the fascists and, on 28 October 1922, Mussolini became the Prime Minister of Italy.

Cementing power

Although Fascist Party rule began as a coalition, Mussolini quickly became a dictator, founding a secret police force, the 'Blackshirts', to crack down on political opponents. In 1926 a new law made Mussolini answerable only to the king. In 1928 another law banned opposition parties altogether and replaced parliamentary elections with votes in which electors were given a list of pre-approved candidates from which to make their choice.

Above: *Mussolini (centre) poses with fascist supporters during the march on Rome in 1922.*

FASCIST VISION

Fascists believed in nationalism and aimed to unite a country's people into a disciplined force under their all-powerful leader. In Italy, the fascist state promoted its values through culture, sport, architecture, social programmes and improvements to roads and railways. Propaganda films portrayed Mussolini as the saviour of the Italian nation. As time went by these methods were viewed with envy by extremist politicians such as Adolf Hitler in Germany, and carefully copied.

Left: *Fascist propaganda used idealised images of strength, unity and past glory to motivate Italians. 'SPQR' is an abbreviation of the Latin for 'The Senate and People of Rome' – the motto of ancient Rome.*

GERMANY IN THE 1920s

The harsh demands of the Treaty of Versailles and the enormous cost of fighting a long war created economic chaos in Germany. By late 1923 ordinary Germans faced great hardship, needing a wheelbarrow full of money to buy a simple loaf of bread.

Below: Map showing the invasion and occupation of the Ruhr by French and Belgian troops.

A faltering economy

The war reparations demanded by the Treaty of Versailles were set at 132 billion gold marks, or about £6.6 billion (US$34 billion). This was a crippling sum. However, not all of this was due in cash – part was to be paid in materials such as coal and steel. But by 1922 the German economy was in serious trouble, and Britain and France had to grant a six-month freeze on reparation payments. Then early in 1923, Germany was unable to make its coal and steel payments, resulting

in French and Belgian troops occupying the Ruhr industrialised area, taking over mines, factories and steelworks. Angry German workers and civil servants began a campaign of resistance by refusing to carry out orders. Industrial output fell and the German economy began to suffer.

As well as these domestic issues, Germany's exports were being hit hard by foreign nations, who had placed harsh taxes on German goods. Things produced by German factories now couldn't easily be sold abroad, so the money the government would have made from the taxes on these goods also fell. To make matters worse, the German government was spending large amounts of money on public works projects, for example improving power stations and building roads, at a time when revenue from income tax was falling.

Above: Sixty thousand French and Belgian troops occupied Germany's Ruhr industrial heartland in 1923.

Hyperinflation

In order to keep up with the cash portion of the war reparations, Germany began to print more and more money. But the more money the government printed, the less it was actually worth, leading to the worst inflation the world has ever seen. In Germany prices rose and rose while the buying power of the mark became less and less. In 1921 the US dollar had been worth 75 marks; by late 1923 one dollar was worth an incredible 4.2 trillion marks.

Faced with this impossible situation, the German government revalued its currency in November 1923, lopping noughts off the value and printing new money. This action, plus a new reparations payment plan called the 'Dawes Plan', which included large loans from American banks, slowly began to stabilise the German economy. But now a cycle of trans-Atlantic loans and payments meant that Germany was borrowing money from the USA to make payments to other European countries, who in turn used this money to pay their debts to the USA.

CULTURAL LIFE

Despite the economic chaos, Germany's capital Berlin became a cultural powerhouse in the 1920s. The city became famous for Bauhaus art and architecture (1919–33), films such as Fritz Lang's Metropolis *(1927) and music such as Kurt Weill's* Threepenny Opera *(1928). The thriving cultural scene attracted English writers such as WH Auden and Christopher Isherwood, whose novels inspired the musical* Cabaret. *In science, too, Berlin led the world, with Albert Einstein winning the Nobel Prize for Physics while teaching at the University of Berlin in 1921. Berlin's thriving gay and transgender subculture, brutally suppressed by the Nazis in the 1930s, pointed the way for tolerance and diversity elsewhere later in the 20th century.*

Left: German banknotes were almost worthless in 1923 so it was cheaper to burn them than use them to buy fuel.

THE GREAT DEPRESSION

Throughout the 1920s the US economy boomed and Americans began to enjoy a higher standard of living than ever before, many buying consumer goods such as cars and radios for the first time. But in 1929 economic disaster struck, causing hardship for millions.

Stock market crash

The Great Depression began in October 1929 when overvalued share prices crashed in New York. Personal incomes and investments, as well as government tax revenues and company profits, were greatly reduced or lost altogether. Hard-pressed consumers cut back on spending and as a result industry slumped, investment and profits dried up and jobs began to disappear.

Mass unemployment

By 1933 unemployment in the USA had reached 25 per cent. People without jobs were unable to repay loans or afford housing, so thousands became homeless. Those with savings tried to withdraw them, placing a severe strain on the US banking system; more than 5,000 banks failed. The unemployed travelled about looking for jobs, depending on homeless shelters and soup kitchens for survival.

Right: Unemployed men queue for food outside a soup kitchen during the Great Depression.

A New Deal

Things began to improve in the USA during 1933, when a new president, Franklin Delano Roosevelt, was elected. Roosevelt promised a 'New Deal', with more government spending to create jobs as well as financial reforms and social security programmes. By 1936 unemployment had fallen to 11 per cent. But a further nosedive in 1937–38 demonstrated that hard times were never very far away.

WORLDWIDE EFFECTS

With so many economies dependent on the USA, the Great Depression caused financial chaos around the world. Here are two examples:

Germany

American banks had been financing Germany's war reparation payments and supporting its economy with loans since the mid-1920s. This support dried up as a result of the Great Depression; by 1932 German unemployment had reached 30 per cent. This new German economic crisis created more support for the Nazi Party, with its promises to get people back to work. Once in power the Nazis cut wages, took control of labour unions and increased military spending, ignoring the Treaty of Versailles. By 1935 German unemployment had fallen but, with Nazi policy dependent on territorial expansion, Europe was on the road to another war.

Great Britain

The Great Depression hit when Britain's economy still had not recovered from the vast expense of fighting the First World War. With fewer markets in which to sell goods, Britain's exports fell by 50 per cent, causing industry to slump. In some northern cities dependent on heavy industry, unemployment reached 70 per cent. Organisations such as the communist-led National Unemployed Workers' Movement sponsored demonstration marches in 1932–33, and the Jarrow Hunger March of 1936 saw unemployed workers from the north march on London to demand government relief. Although these marches achieved little at the time, they paved the way for some of the social reforms enacted in Britain after the Second World War (1939–1945).

Left: This 1932 election propaganda poster reads: 'Our Last Hope: Hitler'. The Nazi Party appealed to many unemployed Germans.

ANTI-SEMITISM IN GERMANY

The onset of the worldwide depression at the end of the 1920s had led to even more hardship within Germany. Many Germans wanted a scapegoat to blame for their country's defeat in the First World War, their economic problems and loss of world power. This led to a resurgence of anti-Semitism, or hatred of Jews.

Jewish history

The Jewish people originally came from the area today known as Israel and Palestine at the eastern end of the Mediterranean over three thousand years ago. In the pre-Christian Roman Empire Jews were tolerated, but when Christianity was made the official religion of the Empire in CE 380, Jews began to be mistrusted and attacked. Christians viewed Jews as the people who had killed Jesus Christ. By the Middle Ages Jews living in European kingdoms such as England, France and Germany were persecuted, massacred or expelled.

In the mid-1800s many European countries, including Germany, granted Jewish people religious and political freedom. This meant that Jews could now work freely in business, medicine and the arts, and many grew rich. But this in turn led to resentment of their success. For poorer Jews living in places such as Russia, life remained precarious. Most lived in ghettos, or closed communities, and persecution was never far away. The assassination of Tsar Alexander II in 1881 led to persecutions after Jews were wrongly blamed for his death; millions of Jews fled to the USA, Britain, South Africa and elsewhere.

Above: *Persecutions in Russia and elsewhere in the 1800s meant that millions of Jews were forced to leave their homes and move elsewhere.*

Jews in Germany

Within Germany Jewish people had been viewed as a threat to society since at least the 1800s. The term 'anti-Semitism' was first coined in an anti-Jewish pamphlet written by the German journalist Wilhelm Marr, in 1879. In 1881, 225,000 Germans signed a petition to the German chancellor, Otto von Bismarck, calling for the 'liberation' of Germans from 'Jewish domination'. However, many liberal Germans objected to anti-Semitism; anti-Semitic political parties only gained four per cent of the vote in 1898 elections. But by 1907 anti-Semitism was a growing problem; 16 anti-Semitic members were elected to the German Parliament.

Discontent and extremism

By the early 1930s the political and economic situation in Germany was desperate. Many discontented Germans came to believe that the reason their country had been forced to accept the humiliating terms of the Treaty of Versailles more than ten years earlier was that it had been 'stabbed in the back', or betrayed, by 'enemies of the state' such as Jews and communists. Extreme political parties came into being to exploit this discontent. One of the most notable was the National Socialist Workers' Party – or the Nazis – led by Adolf Hitler.

Above: Marr's pamphlet suggested that Germans and Jews were locked in conflict – and that the Jews were winning.

Above: During the 1930s, Nazi propaganda used existing German anti-Semitic stereotypes to spread hatred. This poster advertises an anti-Semitic exhibition called The Eternal Jew, organised by the Nazis in 1937.

THE NAZIS COME TO POWER

The National Socialist Workers' Party, or Nazis, was just one of the political parties that arose in the chaos that was Germany after the First World War. They eventually took control of Germany and led the world into another total war.

The rise of Hitler

Adolf Hitler was born in Austria in 1889. He served with the German army in the First World War and was wounded on the Western Front. After the war, Hitler became well known as a political organiser and public speaker. He soon took control of the National Socialist Workers' Party and built up its strength through meetings and rallies, appealing to voters with extreme German nationalist, anti-communist and anti-Semitic views. In 1923 Hitler tried to take over the government in a coup, but this attempt failed and he spent time in prison.

Once released from jail, Hitler concentrated on gaining power legally. He founded groups such as the SA (see box) and, later, the Hitler Youth, to attract new party members, and exploited grievances against the existing government to attract support. This tactic paid off after 1929 when the German economy collapsed during the worldwide economic depression.

Taking power

In 1930, the Nazis won 6.5 million votes in the election (18 per cent of the total), rising to more than 13 million (37 per cent) in 1932. By now Germany needed the Nazis to govern as they had the largest portion of the vote and there were no other serious options available. But Hitler refused to share power and insisted he be made Chancellor (prime minister). On 30 January 1933, President Paul Hindenburg asked Hitler to form a new government and the Nazis were in power.

Left: A portrait photograph of Adolf Hitler taken in the 1920s.

Oppression

In February 1933 the German Reichstag (parliament) burnt down. The government blamed communists for the crime but had actually started the fire themselves in order to give Hitler the excuse he needed to ban all opposition parties. With the passing of the Enabling Act in March, Hitler became a dictator. The Nazis established the Gestapo, or secret state police, whose members had the power to arrest and imprison anyone considered to be an enemy of the state. The first concentration camp, at Dachau near Munich, was built to hold these political prisoners – Roma people, homosexuals, Jews and others.

Nazi beliefs

Nazism was an extreme version of fascism developed by Adolf Hitler, who set forth his beliefs in the book *Mein Kampf* (My Struggle), which he wrote in prison. In it he stated that Aryans – as he called blond-haired northern Europeans such as the Germans – were a 'master race' that was engaged in a permanent struggle with the Jews. Hitler believed that the Jews wanted to destroy the purity of the Aryan race and dominate the world. The only way the German people could survive was to kill the Jews then expand their homeland to create *lebensraum* (living room) to the east of Germany.

Above: The German Reichstag burns on 27 February 1933.

Right: Thousands attended elaborate rallies to hear Hitler and other Nazis speak in stirring terms about their vision of Germany's great future.

SPREADING THE MESSAGE

Hitler and his fellow Nazis were masters of propaganda and manipulation, using violence, bullying and scare tactics in order to intimidate any opposition. The Nazi paramilitary force, the SA *Sturmabteilung* or 'Brownshirts', played a key role in Hitler's rise to power. They protected the Nazis' elaborate rallies and fought with opponents such as communist party members. Eventually the SA evolved into the SS, the feared and fanatical Nazi elite troops of the Second World War.

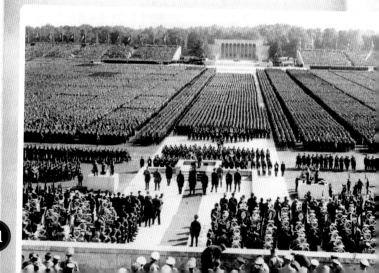

STALIN'S SOVIET UNION

The Bolshevik revolution established a communist government in Russia. But after Lenin's death in 1924, Soviet politics became dominated by one man, who by the 1930s had acquired dictatorial powers. That man was Stalin.

Left: A photo of Stalin taken around the time he joined the Bolshevik Party.

Man of steel

Born in 1878 in Georgia, then part of Tsarist Russia, Iosif Dzhugashvili joined the Bolshevik Party in 1903. He quickly rose through the ranks and was a good organiser. Fiercely anti-Tsarist, Dzhugashvili adopted the name Stalin, meaning 'man of steel', becoming known as a 'hard man' who helped ensure the flow of money to the Bolshevik Party through criminal activity.

By 1917 Stalin had become a member of the Politburo – the group of seven Bolsheviks, led by Lenin, who directed and managed the October Revolution (see pages 16–17). As General Secretary, Stalin expanded his political role throughout the 1920s by repeatedly crushing his opponents and by the 1930s wielded near-absolute power. Soviet propaganda depicted him as the saviour and father of the Soviet Union – cities were named after him, films and poetry idolised him and he assumed grand titles such as 'Father of Nations' and 'Great Architect of Communism'.

Change of plan

Following the end of the civil war in 1923 the Russian economy had all but collapsed. Lenin's New Economic Plan had aimed to restore the country's fortunes through an economy that put the central government in control of important sectors such as industry but allowed private individuals to own small enterprises. These plans were swept away by Stalin, who favoured a highly centralised economy where decisions were taken at the top and no private ownership was allowed. A series of ambitious 'Five-Year Plans', instituted in 1928, laid down goals for the Soviet Union's economic progress.

Collectivisation

Stalin used grain shortages in 1927 as an excuse to implement a forced 'collectivisation' programme that merged small farms into enormous, state-run enterprises. The Soviet government thought this would increase the nation's food supply because the collective farms would be able to afford farm machinery. But this policy, part of which forced farmers to supply nearly all the food they produced to factory workers living in cities, helped to create a devastating famine in 1932–33 when starvation in the Ukraine, Caucasus and other rural regions killed up to eight million people.

Successes

Under Stalin's leadership the Soviet Union experienced achievements in science, engineering and industry and projected an image of itself as an advanced and progressive state. There were also advances in education and healthcare; for example, girls were given a state education and hospital-based pre-natal care was introduced for all women.

Above: *Soviet propaganda promoted the benefits of collectivisation – state-run farms. However, in the early years, the programme resulted in widespread famine.*

'ENEMIES OF THE PEOPLE'

Stalin's regime employed terror tactics to rid itself of millions of opponents from the mid-1930s, using a secret police force to deal with those it branded 'enemies of the people'. Some individuals were tried by committees and executed within 24 hours; others were given long sentences in a network of forced labour camps – the infamous 'gulags' – where prisoners were worked to death on projects such as building canals and roads. Historians estimate that around 700,000 people were killed in 1937–38 alone, with Stalin personally approving the deaths of 40,000 people.

Above: *Soviet 'enemies of the state' were sent to infamous prison camps – gulags – like this one.*

SPANISH CIVIL WAR

Throughout the late 1800s and early 1900s Spain, which had once controlled a huge worldwide empire, experienced political upheaval as Republicans and Nationalists competed for power. In 1936 war broke out when army leaders staged a military coup against the Republican government. Both sides in the war were supported by foreign governments directly, or secretly, who used the conflict to promote their own political agendas.

Background

Spain had remained neutral during the First World War and in 1936 was ruled by the Republican, left-wing government. This had been formed in 1931 when voters elected large numbers of Republican socialists. The Republicans were opposed by Nationalists, supporters of a right-wing political movement called Falangism, which, like fascism, promoted strong authoritarian rule. The stage was set for violent conflict.

The Spanish Civil War, 1936–39

War began in 1936 when a group of right-wing Nationalist officers in the Spanish armed forces issued a *pronunciamento*, or declaration of opposition, to the Republican government. Led by General Francisco Franco, Nationalist army units staged an uprising against the Republican government. However, they were unable to quickly capture many key cities and towns and so Spain descended into civil war.

Left: General Francisco Franco led right-wing forces in the Spanish Civil War and eventually became Spain's leader.

Foreign intervention

Despite official policies of non-intervention adopted by governments such as Britain and France, both sides in the Spanish Civil War were assisted by non-Spanish forces. Left-wing Republicans were secretly supported by Stalin and the Soviet Union, who ignored a League of Nations ban by quietly shipping aircraft, tanks, guns and other weapons to them. In addition, the Republican cause was strengthened by members of the International Brigades – unofficially organised volunteer troops from countries such as Britain,

Left: The city of Guernica in ruins after the air raids in 1937.

Ireland, Canada, the USA and France. These people believed that the Spanish Republic represented the front line in the war against fascism and were willing to risk their lives to try and stop its advance.

Nationalist forces were strongly and openly supported by Nazi Germany, who sent the 'Condor Legion' – a military, combined operations force. Equipped with the latest technology, the Nazis used the conflict as a testing ground for new weapons such as their Ju87 Stuka dive bomber aircraft. They also trialled tactics such as aerial bombardment, attacking the city of Guernica in 1937 and killing up to 300 civilians. Italy, too, supported the Nationalists, supplying weapons, troops and naval forces to assist their cause.

Progress of the war

As the civil war continued, Nationalist troops began to advance from their strongholds in southwest Spain. They captured most of the northern coast in 1937 and besieged, but failed to take Madrid, which remained under Republican control. However, the capture of the Catalonia region in 1938–39 proved a turning point and by 1939 the Nationalists had won the war. Franco then ruled Spain as a dictator until his death in 1975.

The war had been vicious and bloody. Both sides committed atrocities in a foreshadowing of the war crimes of the Second World War and beyond. Nationalists attempted to cleanse Spain of Republican sympathisers, and thousands of left-wing Spaniards were sent into exile or fled for their own safety. The Nationalists also massacred Republican supporters, with thousands of victims buried in mass graves.

Above: Refugees flee Spain in 1939. Half a million Republican sympathisers fled to safety in France after the Nationalists won the war.

WAR IN ASIA

Like Italy, Japan had joined the Allies in the First World War and had been unhappy with its post-war settlement. By the 1930s, Japan's strong military and expansionist policies meant that it was on the road to war with its neighbours and, ultimately, the rest of the world.

Militarisation

Japan had experienced a period of rapid industrial growth in the late 1800s. Japan's leaders, inspired by the success of Prussia, began to build up the country's military. This policy proved successful in the First Sino-Japanese War of 1894–95, in which Japanese troops took control of Korea from Imperial China, and the Russo-Japanese War of 1904–05, when Japan inflicted a humiliating defeat on Tsarist Russia. This latter conflict demonstrated that Japan was now a strong military force, capable of defeating one of the world's great imperial powers.

Resentment and hostility

By the 1920s members of the Japanese armed forces occupied key roles in government and were able to influence its policies. Fascist-style nationalism was also on the rise, fuelled by events such as the USA passing the Japanese Exclusion Act in 1924, which severely limited Japanese immigration to the USA. The onset of the Great Depression in 1929 led to hardship in Japan as protective trade barriers set up by other countries to protect their industries hit exports. Japanese goods became hard to sell abroad, causing Japan's economy to collapse. Resentment and hostility grew against Western countries as nationalists in the armed forces gradually took control of the Japanese government.

Left: A triumphant Japanese painting of Japanese forces during the Russo-Japanese War of 1904-05.

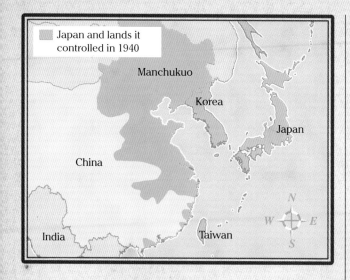

Above: This map shows the extent of Japan's control of northern China and Korea in 1940.

Expansion and conflict

Lack of raw materials, such as coal and iron ore, was a big problem for Japanese industry. Japan's leaders, therefore, began to eye neighbouring Manchuria – a vast province in northern China – as a possible source of these key materials, as well as a market for Japanese goods. In 1931 Japanese forces invaded the region, eventually setting up a new state, which they called Manchukuo. China, weakened by civil war and unable to fight Japan directly, appealed for help to the League of Nations, which declared that Manchuria officially belonged to China. Japan withdrew from the league in protest.

The Sino-Japanese War

In July 1937, Japanese and Chinese troops exchanged shots on either side of the Marco Polo Bridge near Beijing. This event soon escalated into a full-scale war that saw Japanese forces invade northern and central regions of China. The ruthlessness and cruelty of Japanese troops reached a climax in the Chinese city of Nanjing, which fell on 13 December. Here, up to 300,000 civilians were brutally raped, tortured and massacred in an orgy of violence that lasted six weeks. In 1938 Japan announced a 'New Order' in eastern Asia, dominated by itself. This set the stage for Japan's attack on the USA at Pearl Harbor in 1941 and its further military expansion throughout the Pacific region during the Second World War.

THE ANTI-COMINTERN PACT

In November 1936, Nazi Germany signed an alliance with Japan known as the Anti-Comintern Pact. This was directed at their mutual enemy, the Soviet Union. The two nations agreed to consult with each other to 'safeguard their common interests' in the event of a Soviet attack. Germany also recognised Japan's puppet state, Manchukuo. Italy joined the pact in 1937.

Above: During the Sino-Japanese War, the Chinese city of Chongqing was devastated by repeated air raids that killed more than 10,000 civilians.

THE ROAD TO WAR

With the Nazis firmly in power, Germany's expansionist agenda quickly became clear. Some people believed that if the Nazis were appeased – or given concessions – Hitler would be satisfied. Others, however, began to believe that the only way to stop the Nazis was to stand fast and prepare for the inevitable war.

Rhineland crisis

By 1936 Hitler was quickly rebuilding the German war machine. On 7 March German troops reoccupied the Rhineland (see map, page 24), which had been demilitarised under the terms of the Treaty of Versailles. The Nazis had been planning this action ever since taking power in 1933. The introduction of Nazi troops to the Rhineland shifted the balance of power in Europe from France towards Germany by removing a key 'buffer zone' between the two nations.

Fascist Italy had also been expanding its territory, invading the east African nation of Abyssinia (Ethiopia) in 1935–36. The League of Nations called for economic sanctions but Italy ignored these and quit the league as Germany had done in 1933.

The Axis

Hitler had supported the idea of an alliance between Nazi Germany and Italy since the 1920s. In November 1936, with Italy in trouble over its African aggression, Germany and Italy signed a pact known as the 'Rome-Berlin' Axis. The signing of the Anti-Comintern Pact later that month between Germany and Japan confirmed the key 'Axis Powers' of the coming war.

Left: German troops march across the bridge at Cologne to reoccupy the Rhineland in 1936.

Anschluss

On 12 March 1938 Germany invaded Austria, an action that Nazi propaganda portrayed as an *Anschluss* (union) of Germanic peoples. In reality Hitler had sent troops to enforce in the Nazis' favour the result of a vote by Austrians on whether such a union should take place. The vote was cancelled the day before the Nazi invasion, but held the following month when the Nazis claimed 99 per cent of voters favoured union with Germany. Jews were not allowed to vote.

Although a union between Germany and Austria had been specifically forbidden by the Treaty of Versailles, reaction from the Allied powers was only verbal and moderate. It seemed that no one wanted to provoke a confrontation with the war machine that was Nazi Germany.

Above: Nazi supporters parade Nazi flags through Vienna, Austria, during the Anschluss in 1938.

THE MUNICH CRISIS

After Austria, the Nazis began to focus on Czechoslovakia, a country once part of Austria-Hungary. Hitler threatened to invade unless Germany was allowed to take over Czechoslovakia's industrial Sudetenland border region. The leaders of Britain, France and Italy attended a conference in Munich in September where they agreed to the Nazis' demands. The Czechoslovakians were not consulted or even invited to the conference.

British Prime Minister Neville Chamberlain described Nazi aggression in Czechoslovakia as 'a quarrel in a faraway country between people of whom we know nothing', and announced that he had secured 'peace for our time'. But some politicians realised that the Nazis were not going to be stopped by concessions. In March 1939 Nazi forces invaded western Czechoslovakia, and worse was to come.

Above: Neville Chamberlain waves the Munich Agreement after stepping off the plane at Heston Aerodrome on 30 September 1938.

KRISTALLNACHT

Throughout the 1930s life became very difficult for German Jews. Many began to flee, seeking a new life in Britain, the USA and elsewhere. Nazi anti-Jewish hatred reached a peak on *Kristallnacht* in 1938, when Jewish homes, businesses and synagogues were attacked and vandalised.

Attacks on Jews

As the Nazis became more powerful, attacks on Jews increased. Gangs of SA stormtroopers looted shops and burned synagogues. A one-day boycott of Jewish businesses took place on 1 April 1933 and later, books written by Jewish and other 'unacceptable' authors were burned publicly in Berlin. Jews were fired from their jobs in the civil service, the law, schools and universities; actors and musicians were forbidden to perform.

Increasing persecution

By May 1935 the situation for German Jews became even more terrible when the Defence Law excluded them from the armed forces. This was particularly harsh, as German Jews had fought with great courage during the First World War. However worse was to come as, in September, the Nuremburg Laws stripped Jews of their German citizenship and banned them from marrying Germans.

  The Nuremburg Laws defined who the Nazis considered to be a Jew, setting out degrees of Jewishness based on the number of Jewish grandparents a person had. In

Above: Throughout Nazi-occupied Europe, Jews were forced to wear a Star of David on their clothes to identify them as Jews.

1936 Nazi persecution continued – those who had not already lost their professions were no longer permitted to work as teachers, vets or tax consultants.

Kristallnacht

The Nazi persecution against German Jews reached a climax on 9–10 November 1938. Hirschel Grynszpan, a German Jew protesting against the fact that his parents had been forced to leave Germany, shot an official at the German Embassy in Paris. In Germany reaction was swift. More than 7,500 Jewish shops were attacked, synagogues burned and Jewish graveyards vandalised. Kristallnacht means 'night of the broken glass' and the name of this event refers to the fact that German streets were strewn with glass from smashed Jewish shop windows. More than 90 Jews were killed on Kristallnacht; around 30,000 Jewish men were rounded up and held in concentration camps, where many died from the brutal treatment they suffered.

Above: Across Germany around 250 synagogues and 7,000 Jewish businesses were vandalised and looted on Kristallnacht.

THE KINDERTRANSPORT

On 15 November 1938, only a few days after Kristallnacht, a delegation of British Jewish and Quaker leaders appealed to Prime Minister Neville Chamberlain to allow Jewish children under threat from the Nazis to flee to safety in Britain. A few days later, the British government passed a bill suspending normal immigration rules for unaccompanied refugee children.

The first Kindertransport (children's transport) train left Berlin on 1 December 1938 and the final one left on 1 September 1939, the day that the Second World War began. Between those dates, nearly 10,000 Jewish children were moved from Germany and other Nazi-occupied countries by brave volunteers and were placed in foster homes and hostels.

Below: Most of the children travelled by rail to the Netherlands and then by boat and train to London's Liverpool Street Station, where today a memorial commemorates their arrival.

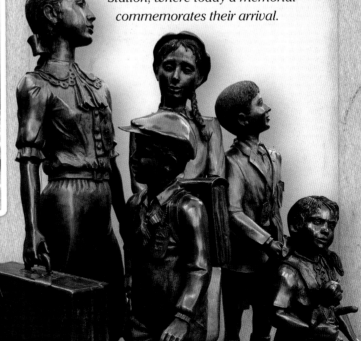

WAR AGAIN

By summer 1939 another war in Europe was looming. Germany had taken over Austria and Czechoslovakia; now Hitler focused on Poland.

Poland

After the occupation of Czechoslovakia, Germany demanded the free city of Danzig on the Baltic Sea. Danzig was officially neutral and under the protection of the League of Nations. Germany also wanted to access its province of East Prussia through the corridor of land that linked Poland to the Baltic. Poland refused these demands so Germany prepared to invade. By this time Britain and France had finally realised that there was no point in trying to offer Hitler any more concessions, so they promised Poland support if Germany invaded.

The Nazi-Soviet pact

To successfully invade Poland, Hitler needed to reach an agreement with Poland's neighbour to the east, Soviet Russia. Therefore, on 23 August 1939, a 'non-aggression pact' was signed between Germany and the Soviet Union. The pact included the promise that neither country would go to war with each other. It also included a secret agreement that would divide Poland between Germany and the Soviet Union and allow the latter to occupy Finland, the Baltic states and, later, eastern Romania. This pact remained in force until Germany invaded the Soviet Union in 1941.

Invasion

On 1 September, Nazi forces invaded Poland. When they refused to withdraw, Britain, France and their empires declared war. The Polish army was overwhelmed by a combination of aerial bombardment and a rapid motorised advance known as *blitzkrieg* (lightning war). Russia invaded Poland from the east on 17 September. The Second World War – a titanic struggle against fascism and oppression – had begun.

Left: *This cartoon makes fun of the Nazi-Soviet pact by showing Hitler and Stalin getting married.*

Left: Hitler salutes his troops as they march into Poland, September 1939.

Below: The two atomic bombs dropped on Japan in 1945 killed at least 130,000 people instantly, with thousands more dying of radiation sickness.

Aftermath

War raged around the world for six long years, causing untold suffering and between 70 to 85 million deaths. These included soldiers who died in battle as well as civilians killed by military action, famine and disease. Around six million Jews were systematically murdered in Nazi concentration camps. At the end of the war the use of the most deadly weapon ever invented – the atomic bomb – ushered in decades of worldwide 'cold war' between the Soviet Union and the west, along with stockpiles of nuclear missiles.

The Second World War ended in 1945 with the total defeat of the Axis powers. But this time there was to be no Treaty of Versailles. British Prime Minister Winston Churchill promoted a spirit of co-operation rather than revenge, and both Germany and Japan – as well as many war-shattered European countries – were given financial help to rebuild after the war.

THE UNITED NATIONS

A replacement for the ineffective League of Nations, the United Nations (UN) was founded in 1945 in order to help prevent war. The organisation had 51 member states at its creation; now there are 193. Unlike the League of Nations, the UN has the ability to deploy peacekeeping troops, drawn from the armed forces of member states, to help defuse trouble.

MAPS

This map shows European country boundaries in 1914.

This map shows Europe post-1919, with boundaries re-shaped by the First World War.

TIMELINE

28 June 1914 Assassination of Archduke Franz Ferdinand in Sarajevo, Bosnia (formerly part of Serbia but annexed by Austria-Hungary).

28 July 1914 Austria-Hungary declares war on Serbia; Russia mobilises its armed forces against Austria-Hungary.

1 August 1914 Germany declares war on Russia.

3 August 1914 Germany declares war on France.

4 August 1914 Germany invades Belgium; Great Britain declares war on Germany.

6 April 1917 The United States declares war on Germany.

February/March 1917 The first Russian revolution creates a provisional government in Russia.

October/November 1917 The October Revolution led by Lenin; Bolsheviks seize power.

8 January 1918 US President Woodrow Wilson outlines his 'Fourteen Points'.

3 March 1918 The Treaty of Brest-Litovsk ends Russia's involvement in the First World War.

1918–1923 Civil war rages in Russia; the Bolsheviks eventually win control.

September 1918 onwards Germany is hit by mutinies and strikes.

3 November 1918 Austria-Hungary signs an armistice with Italy, which takes effect 4 November.

9 November 1918 Kaiser Wilhelm II abdicates; the German Republic is proclaimed.

11 November 1918 Germany signs the Armistice with the Allies; fighting ends; Poland is proclaimed an independent country.

12 November 1918 Austria is proclaimed a republic.

14 November 1918 Czechoslovakia is proclaimed a republic.

18 January 1919–21 January 1920 Paris Peace Conference

25 January 1919 Proposal to create the League of Nations is accepted.

28 June 1919 Treaty of Versailles signed; other treaties with former member of the Central Powers follow.

July 1920 British mandate in Palestine begins.

27-28 October 1922 Fascist march on Rome; Mussolini becomes Italian Prime Minister.

1921 Adolf Hitler becomes leader of NSDAP, the forerunner of the Nazi Party.

1923 German economy in chaos, hit by hyperinflation; French and Belgian troops occupy the Ruhr; Hitler attempts to seize power and serves one year in prison.

1924 German reparation payments rescheduled; US banks lend money to assist.

1924 Stalin begins to consolidate power in the Soviet Russia.

May 1926 General Strike in Britain.

1927 Grain shortages in Soviet Union; collectivisation programme begins.

October 1929 Share prices crash in the USA; the Great Depression begins.

1931 Japanese forces invade Manchuria.

1932-33 Famine in Soviet Union, partially caused by Stalin's collectivisation policy; mass marches by workers in Britain demanding social relief.

1933 Nazis gain power in Germany; Enabling Act makes Hitler a dictator; Germany withdraws from League of Nations; Roosevelt elected president in USA.

1935 Italy invades Abyssinia; Italy quits League of Nations; Defence Law in Germany excludes Jews from armed forces; Nuremburg Laws strip Jews of German citizenship.

1936 Germany occupies the Rhineland; Spanish Civil War; alliance signed between Germany and Italy; Anti-Comintern Pact signed between Germany and Japan; Jarrow Hunger March in Britain.

1937 Sino-Japanese War begins; Italy joins Anti-Comintern Pact; further economic slump in USA.

12 March 1938 Germany annexes Austria.

September 1938 Munich Conference; Germany annexes Sudentenland on 10 October.

9-10 November 1938 Kristallnacht attacks on Jewish businesses and synagogues.

1 December 1938–1 September 1939 Kindertransport trains rescue Jewish children from Nazi persecution.

March 1939 Germany invades Czechoslovakia.

1 September 1939 Germany invades Poland; the Second World War begins.

GLOSSARY

Abdicate When a monarch or emperor officially quits and gives up the throne.

Allied powers Britain and its empire, France, the USA and, after 1941, Russia, who opposed the Axis powers during the Second World War.

Ally A country linked with another by treaty or friendship.

Annex Take possession of another country, or part of another country.

Anti-Semitism Prejudice against, or hatred of, Jewish people.

Armistice An agreement between warring nations to stop fighting while a peace deal is worked out.

Axis powers Nazi Germany, Italy, Japan and some other countries, who opposed the Allies during the Second World War.

Blitzkrieg German word meaning 'lightning war', describing the rapid advance of Nazi armed forces during the Second World War.

Bolshevik A member of the radical political party that overthrew the Russian government and established communism in 1917.

Capitalism An economic system based on the private ownership of industry, finance and property.

Ceasefire When warring sides call a temporary halt to fighting, for example to allow humanitarian aid to be delivered.

Coalition An alliance between different political parties in order to form a workable government.

Cold War The campaign of propaganda and opposing beliefs between democratic and communist nations from 1945 to 1990. It was characterised by the build-up, and fear, of nuclear weapons.

Colonial Referring to an empire made up of colonies.

Colony A region or country controlled by another country as part of an empire.

Communism Belief in a society with no social classes, in which everyone is equal and all property is owned and shared by the people.

Concentration camp A camp-like prison where people are held in terrible living conditions. The Nazis established concentration camps in the 1930s to imprison Jews, homosexuals, Roma people and political opponents. During the Second World War, the Nazis turned some of these camps into extermination camps where Jews were murdered in great numbers.

Conscription When a government compels people to join its armed forces to fight in a war.

Corrupt Granting work or jobs in return for money payments or because of family connections.

Coup To overthrow a country's government by force.

Delegation A group of officials appointed by a government to do something, for example to sign a treaty or attend a conference.

Demilitarise Official action to remove soldiers and weapons from a region, usually to create a 'buffer zone' between two bitter enemies.

Democracy Government by the people or by their elected representatives, often taking the form of political parties with opposing views.

Depression An extreme economic downturn when money and credit become scarce, exports slump, people lose their jobs and often their homes.

Dictator A leader who takes complete control of a country, usually ruling by force.

Economic sanctions Financial punishments imposed on countries who take actions contrary to international law.

Elected assembly A body made up of representatives elected by voters, and which makes laws on their behalf.

Elite A group that is set apart from, or above, ordinary people by birth, training or skills.

Empire A group of different nations and peoples, ruled by one nation and its emperor.

Expansionist Policies aimed at increasing a country's area.

Fascism An extreme political movement based on nationalism and authority, often military, which aims to unite a country's people into a disciplined force under an all-powerful leader.

Genocide When one portion of a society attempts to systematically murder another group that is ethnically distinct from it.

Holocaust The Nazis' mass murder of European Jews during the Second World War.

Howitzer A large field gun used to fire explosive shells.

Income tax Money payments made to a government that are based on how much a person earns.

Industrialisation When a country begins to build many factories to produce goods and changes its economy from one based on farming to one based on manufacturing.

League of Nations An organisation set up in 1919, which tried to solve disputes between countries.

Left wing Tending towards socialist or communist political views.

Liberal Tending towards moderate political views; neither left nor right wing.

Mandate Here, an authority given to a nation to manage a newly created country until a proper government can be set up there.

National debt The total amount of money a government borrows to fund its laws, social programmes such as housing, armed forces etc.

Nationalist Someone who is extremely loyal and devoted to his or her country.

Nazi A member of Adolf Hitler's National Socialist Workers' Party, which held extreme fascist beliefs and ruled Germany from 1933-45.

Neutral A nation that refuses to take sides in a war and doesn't fight.

Offensive A carefully planned military attack made by a large number of soldiers.

Ottoman Empire An empire based in Turkey that existed from the Middle Ages to 1922–23 and which controlled much of the Middle East. The Ottoman Empire joined with Germany and Austria-Hungary during the First World War.

Propaganda Information spread by a country's government to make people think a certain way or to influence their opinions.

Puppet state A state that is supposedly independent but in fact is the creation of an outside power.

Rally Here, a large public event held by a political party to whip up support and encourage people to join its cause.

Red Army The army of Soviet Russia.

Renounce To no longer support a previous agreement, such as a treaty.

Reparation Money a nation has to pay to compensate former enemies for wartime damage.

Republic A country ruled by an elected head of state, such as a president.

Revolution A total, and normally violent, overthrow of a country's government and institutions.

Right wing Tending towards conservative, capitalist or nationalist political views.

Ruhr The area of north-west Germany, near the River Ruhr, known for its coal mines and industries.

Scapegoat Someone, usually innocent, who is forced to take the blame for a situation.

Socialism A political system in which people may own property, but important industries and resources are managed by the government on behalf of the people, and where there also exists a welfare system to assist the disadvantaged.

Theatre of war The area of air, land and sea where fighting takes place in a war.

Total war A war involving every aspect of a country's military, economic and industrial resources.

Treaty A formal agreement between nations.

Tsar An emperor of Russia.

White Army The army made up of monarchist and liberal forces that opposed the communist Red Army during the Russian Civil War of 1918–23.

Zionist Someone who favoured the creation of a Jewish homeland in Palestine.

INDEX